D0190282

POSITIVE STEPS

Respecting Others

Susan Martineau

with illustrations by Hel James

W
FRANKLIN WATTS
LONDON·SYDNEY

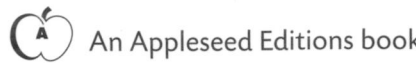 An Appleseed Editions book

First published in 2011 by Franklin Watts
338 Euston Road, London NW1 3BH

Franklin Watts Australia
Hachette Children's Books
Level 17/207 Kent St, Sydney, NSW 2000

© 2011 Appleseed Editions

Created by Appleseed Editions Ltd,
Well House, Friars Hill, Guestling,
East Sussex TN35 4ET

Designed and illustrated by Hel James
Edited by Mary-Jane Wilkins
Picture research by Su Alexander

ISBN 978-1-4451-0364-8

Dewey Classification 177.7

A CIP catalogue for this book is available from the British Library.

Picture credits
All photographs from Shutterstock.
Contents page Zurijeta; 4 Gelpi; 5 Vinicius Tupinamba 6 Dmitriy Shironosov;
7l Ivan Pavlisko, r Forster Forest; 9 Benis Arapovic; 11t Mandy Godbehear,
b John Steel; 12 Monkey Business Images; 13 Beata Becla; 14 Morgan Lane
Photography; 15 Zurijeta; 16 (main image) Bluefox; (inset) Zurijeta; 17t Monkey
Business Images, b Hirurg, background Hal_P; 19 Fotoksa; 20 StockLite; 21 AXL;
22 Alexander Chaikin; 23t ZQFotography, bl Wawritto, br Tischenko Irina;
24 Sklep Spozywczy; 26 Filip Fuxa; 27l Dmitriy Shironosov, r SergiyN;
28-29 Iakov Kalinin; 32 Margot Petrowski
Front cover Forster Forest

Printed in Singapore

Franklin Watts is a division of Hachette Children's Books,
an Hachette UK company.
www.hachette.co.uk

Contents

I respect my friends.

Thinking of others

When we treat people respectfully we show that we care about how they feel. The things we say or do make a difference to other people. We need to treat our friends, family and other people in the same way as we would like them to treat us.

We need to be careful about how we speak to other people and how we listen to them. **Polite** words such as 'please' and 'thank you' are important, but how you say and do things also matter. You can even have an argument with someone in a respectful way!

LET'S TALK ABOUT...

Look at what these children are saying. They are talking about some ways of showing respect to other people. Can you think of any more? Have a look through the book to see some examples.

Show respect to everyone, not just your friends.

Think of ways you can help other people.

Treating people respectfully shows that we have thought about what they need and how they are feeling.

Please and thank you

Being polite to other people is an important way of showing respect for them. Having good **manners** helps everyone to get along with one another.

Greeting our friends shows them we care for them and how they are feeling. When we ask for something at school, at home or in a shop it is good manners to say 'please'. Don't forget to say 'thank you' too!

6

We should always thank someone when we've been to their house or if they have given us a present.

Sometimes we also need to be able to say 'no' politely. We will not sound **rude** as long as we say, 'no, thank you'!

Thank you for having me.

Thanks for the brilliant present.

Design a card

There are times when you cannot thank someone face to face. You could design your own thank you card. It could be one to send in the post or one to email.

Thank you

The present is great!

THANKS MUM

Making friends

Anna has just moved house to a new town far from her old home. She is writing to her best friend Jasmine.

confused

lonely

excited

nervous

Hi Jas

The new house is great and I love my bedroom. But I'm missing you a lot and I'm really worried about starting my new school next week.

shy

What if I don't make any friends or they don't like me? I'm so scared.

lost!

sad

Write soon. Wish you were here.

Love Anna x

LET'S TALK ABOUT...

How could you help Anna if she was coming to your school? Look at the words on the left. Do they describe how you felt on your first day at school?

What can you do?

If you notice someone looking lost and lonely you could:

- Go and say 'Hi'. Ask them their name.

- Invite them to join in a game.

- Offer to sit with them at lunchtime.

- Help them find their way around.

Can you think of any other ways to be **kind** and show respect to a new person?

I've made loads of new friends.

Listening to others

When we listen politely to other people we show them that we respect them and we want to hear what they are saying. When we meet someone new, we need to listen to them so we can find out about them and get to know them.

Hi, I'm Arun. What's your name?

I'm Jack.

Do you like football?

We should not forget old friends too! They also need to know we are interested in what they say and do, and that we care about how they are feeling.

Listening politely to grown-ups is very important. They might be telling you something that will keep you safe.

LET'S TALK ABOUT...

How do you know if someone is really listening to you? Have a look at the list below and see if you can think of anything else.

They let you finish what you are saying without **interrupting** you.

They look you in the eye when you are talking.

They ask you questions about what you've just said.

The listening game

Everyone gets into pairs with someone they do not usually talk to or play with. Ask each other questions about the games you like best, favourite food or movies. Then take it in turns to **introduce** your partner to the others.

This is Oakley. He's seven years old. His favourite food is doughnuts!

Can I help you?

Helping at school or at home shows that we are thinking about other people. Being **considerate** like this means we are not just thinking about ourselves. We are respecting others.

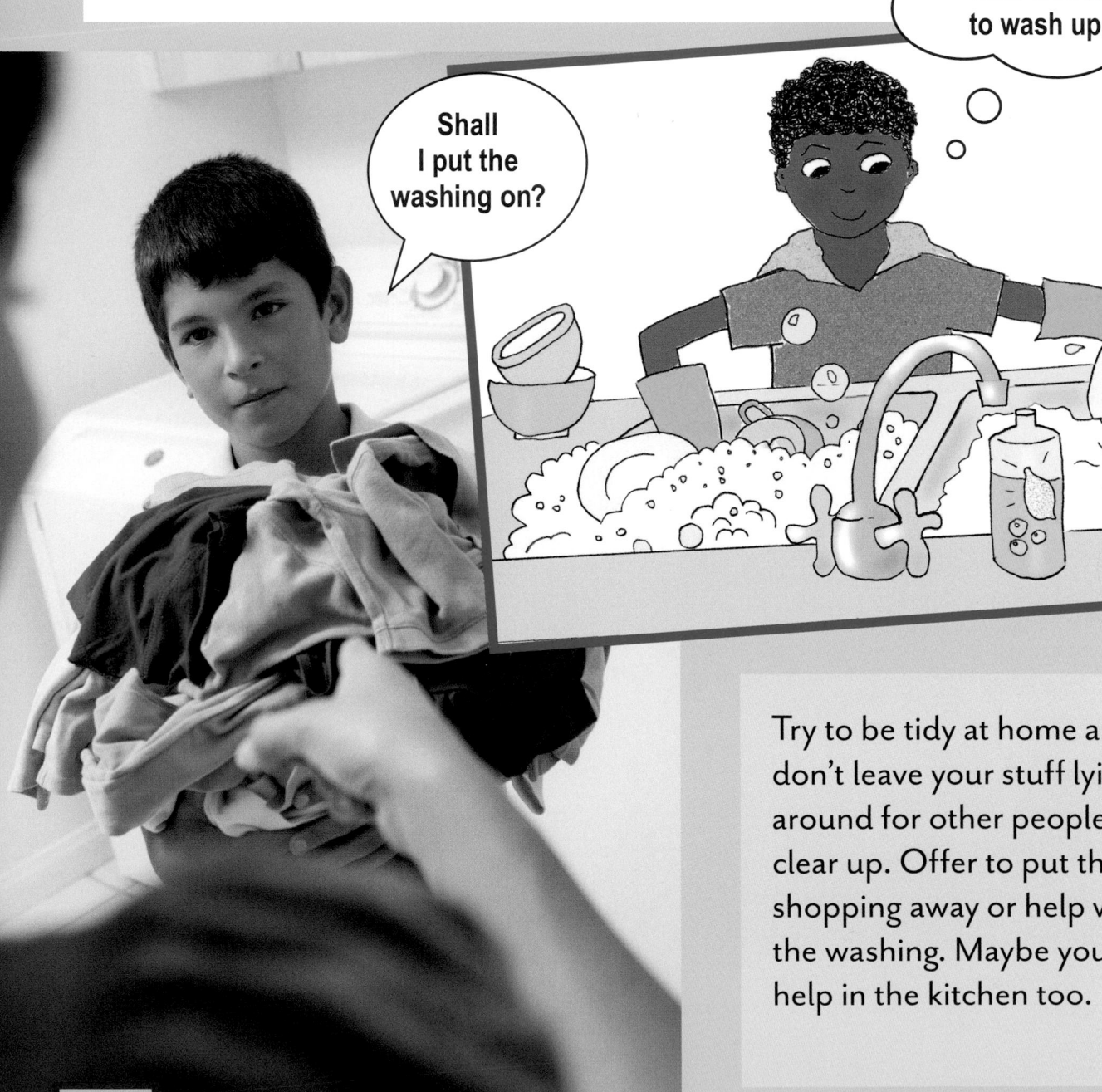

Shall I put the washing on?

Take it in turns to wash up.

Try to be tidy at home and don't leave your stuff lying around for other people to clear up. Offer to put the shopping away or help with the washing. Maybe you can help in the kitchen too.

What can you do?

At school you could offer to tidy the classroom or be on hand to give out books or other things for your teacher.

When we are out and about we also need to think about how our actions make a difference to others. We should always wait our turn in a queue and hold the door open for people behind us.

How I helped on

Monday	put washing away
Tuesday	tidied my room
Wednesday	
Thursday	
Friday	
Saturday	
Sunday	

The helping diary

You could keep a diary of all the things you've done to help at home or at school during the week. Maybe you could even persuade your teacher or family that you deserve a treat when you show them the diary!

It's party time!

Ben is feeling a bit hurt because he was not invited to a party. He is writing to his older cousin about it.

Hi Josh

How are you? I'm OK but I didn't get invited to George's party last week. He told me he was sorry, but his mum said he couldn't invite the whole class.

Look forward to seeing you soon.

Ben

Respecting others means thinking about their feelings, but sometimes it is hard to keep everyone happy. Can you think of a way that George could cheer Ben up? Maybe he could invite Ben over to play another time?

What can you do?

If you are having a party remember to think of other people's feelings. If you can't invite everyone, try not to give out invitations at school in front of everyone. Don't go on about your party in front of anyone you have not invited!

Please don't slurp

Table manners might sound boring, but they do matter. If we eat politely instead of grabbing food or eating with our mouths open it makes meal times nicer for everyone. It shows we respect the other people at the table.

Can you think of times when it's all right to use your hands to eat? Some countries have different ways of eating. For example, in China and Japan people eat food with chopsticks.

When you eat at a friend's house, it is polite to thank them for the meal. Try to eat the food you are given, even if you do not like all of it!

The eating game

Ask your teacher if you can practise setting the table with knives, forks and spoons. Take it in turns to sit down and eat some imaginary food! You could try this eating game with chopsticks too.

17

Having an argument

You stupid idiot!

We all lose our tempers from time to time. We sometimes **disagree** with our friends or don't want to do things their way.

Shouting or being rude to someone is **disrespectful** and so is calling someone rude names or **swearing** at them.

I'm sorry, but I don't really agree with you.

You can disagree with other people in a **calm** and polite way. Then they are also much more likely to listen to your point of view. Try the game on the next page to practise this.

How do you feel if someone shouts or yells at you? You are likely to shout back and then everyone gets even more upset. Can you think of other words to use in a polite argument?

I see what you mean, but...

Yes, but what about...

Don't laugh at what someone says, unless they are making a joke.

The debate game

Take it in turns to speak about swearing. Why do people swear? Is it ever all right to use swear words? Each speaker has a minute to talk and then everyone else can ask them questions.

Listen to each speaker without interrupting.

Speak clearly and politely.

Try to be on time

Being on time, or **punctual**, is good manners and shows that we respect others. Nobody likes to be kept waiting.

We're fed up with you keeping us waiting.

You're late again!

We should always try to be on time, whether we are meeting friends or going to the dentist.

*If you are late and keep others waiting it is like saying that your time is more important than theirs. It is **selfish** and **inconsiderate**. Can you think of times when you have had to wait for someone? How did it make you feel?*

hurt

cross

let down

bored

What can you do?

Take **responsibility** for being on time. Perhaps you could ask for an alarm clock to help you wake up in the morning. When you get ready to meet someone or go to school, keep an eye on the clock or a watch to check that you are going to be punctual.

Don't drop litter!

Please don't drop that. Someone else will have to pick it up.

No one likes to see rubbish lying on the ground. Old crisp packets, sweet wrappers and used drink cartons are **litter**. Litter is dirty and unhealthy and it belongs in the bin!

If we throw our rubbish on the ground it means we do not respect or care about other people or our **environment**.

What can you do?

Check where the bins are in your school. Does everyone know where they are? Maybe you could ask your teacher about **recycling** some of the things you throw away at school. Cardboard and paper can all be recycled. This is good for our environment.

Don't chuck it, bin it!

You could design some posters to put up which remind everyone that they should put their rubbish in the bin!

Put it in the bin

On the phone

Hello?

Hello Anya, could I speak to your mum please?

When we are on the phone we need to speak clearly and listen carefully. Anya is answering the phone at her mum's house.

Anya needs to find out who is calling. Perhaps she could write down the person's number so her mum can call them back.

She can't come to the phone at the moment. Can I take a message?

If someone grunts 'yeah' or 'what?' on the phone it sounds rude! Can you think of some good ways of answering the phone? Remember that you do not have to say your name unless you know the person who is calling. Can you also think of polite things to say when you are making a phone call yourself?

Hello, who's calling please?

Who would you like to speak to?

Hello, please could I speak to Dan?

Hello, it's Holly. Is Martha there please?

Can I take a message?

Play this phone game with as many people as possible. One person 'rings' another and asks if they will pass on a message. The second person then has to 'ring' someone else and pass on the same message. Keep going until you run out of people and see if the message has been passed on correctly!

Having visitors

When our friends or family come to visit us it is good to make them feel welcome by showing them that we are pleased to see them.

Hello Uncle Jim. How are you?

Do you want to come and see the new hamster?

Even if they have come to see everyone else in the house, we should not ignore them or just carry on watching TV when they arrive.

Try to think of something your visitor might like to do.

Great to see you...

Hi!

Do you want some juice?

What can you do?

Visitors will feel at home if you:

- Greet them when they arrive.

- Talk to them and ask them what they would like to do.

- Ask them if they would like something to eat or drink.

Thanks for coming over. Come again soon.

When visitors are about to go, say goodbye to them so that they know you enjoyed seeing them.

Being respectful

Being respectful to others means you care about the way you treat them and you care about what they think of you. There are many ways of being respectful.

Don't be a litter bug!

Be welcoming to visitors or new people.

Sometimes other people are not very respectful towards us. We should still try our best to be respectful towards them.

Be thoughtful and kind.

Respect others as you would like them to respect you.

Look at people when they are talking to you.

What can you do?
Have a look at the bold words in the book. Check that you know what they mean by turning to the Words to know on pages 30-31. Get into pairs and make up some sentences using the words. You can use more than one in the same sentence. Remember to listen to each other!

The **bold** words are explained on pages 30-31.

Words to know

calm
Quiet – not noisy or excited.

considerate
Being considerate means thinking about what other people would like and other people's feelings.

disagree
Not to agree with someone. To think they are wrong.

disrespectful
The opposite of showing someone respect and being considerate.

environment
The world around us.

inconsiderate
Not thinking about others and their feelings. The opposite of considerate.

interrupt
To speak when someone else is talking.

introduce
To tell others about someone else so they can get to know them.

kind
Friendly, considerate and helpful.

litter
Rubbish that has been thrown on the ground.

manners
Having good manners means saying 'please',
'thank you' and 'sorry'.

polite
Having good manners.

punctual
On time.

recycling
Making rubbish into things that can be used again.

responsibility
Taking responsibility means being in charge
of something yourself.

rude
Having bad manners and not being polite.
Sometimes people are rude on purpose.

selfish
Thinking about yourself and not others in the
way you behave.

swearing
Using rude words that might upset people.

Index

Friends care about each other.